Rounds for Children.

Amsco Publications
New York/London/Sydney

Cover art direction by Mike Bell
Cover illustration by Graham Percy
Interior illustrations by Michelle Lyons
Interior layout by Linda Ganus

Order No. AM 60260
US International Standard Book Number: 0.8256.2442.8
UK International Standard Book Number: 0.7119.0863.X

Exclusive Distributors:
Music Sales Corporation
257 Park Avenue South, New York, NY 10010 USA
Music Sales Limited
8/9 Frith Street, London W1V 5TZ England
Music Sales Pty. Limited
120 Rothschild Street, Rosebery, Sydney, NSW 2018, Australia

Printed in the United States of America by
Vicks Lithograph and Printing Corporation

How To Sing A Round

- The singer here is part of an ensemble

- Rhythm is to be strictly adhered to

- It is suggested that the round be individually sung by those taking part to get the feel and rhythmic beat of the song

(Music Example #1)

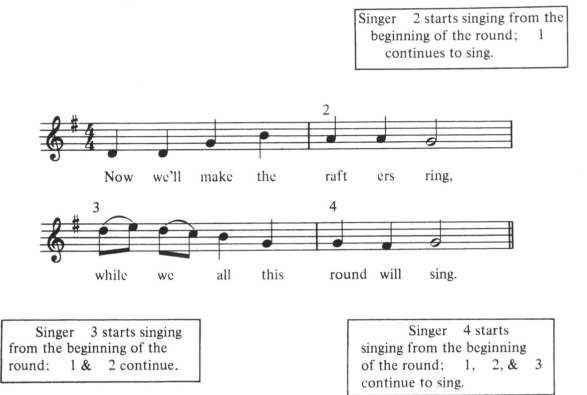

Singer 2 starts singing from the beginning of the round; 1 continues to sing.

Now we'll make the raft ers ring,

while we all this round will sing.

Singer 3 starts singing from the beginning of the round; 1 & 2 continue.

Singer 4 starts singing from the beginning of the round; 1, 2, & 3 continue to sing.

NB: TO STOP SINGING: 1 stops singing at the end of the last bar of music. At this point, 2, 3, and 4 are still singing. Each singer stops in turn at the end of the last bar, so 2 will stop second, 3 third, and 4 last.

(Music Example #2)

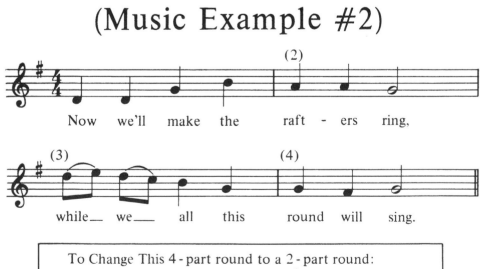

Now we'll make the raft - ers ring,

while__ we__ all this round will sing.

To Change This 4 - part round to a 2 - part round:
Singer #2 starts singing where Singer #3 usually begins; now both parts are equal. Singer #2 could stop at the normal place; in this case, no one starts singing at #3 or #4.

TWO PART ROUNDS

At Summer Morn

At sum - mer morn the mer - ry lark Her - alds in the day;

At e - ven - tide sad Phil - o - mel Breathes her plain - tive lay.

Chit

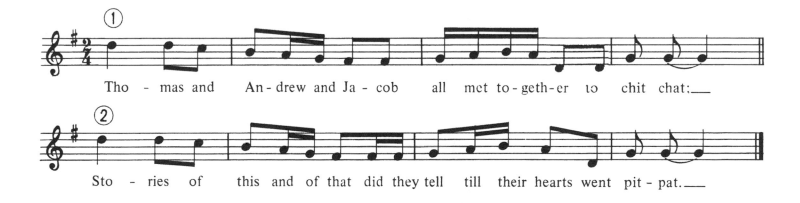

Tho - mas and An - drew and Ja - cob all met to-geth-er to chit chat;

Sto - ries of this and of that did they tell till their hearts went pit - pat.

A Cuckoo And An Owl

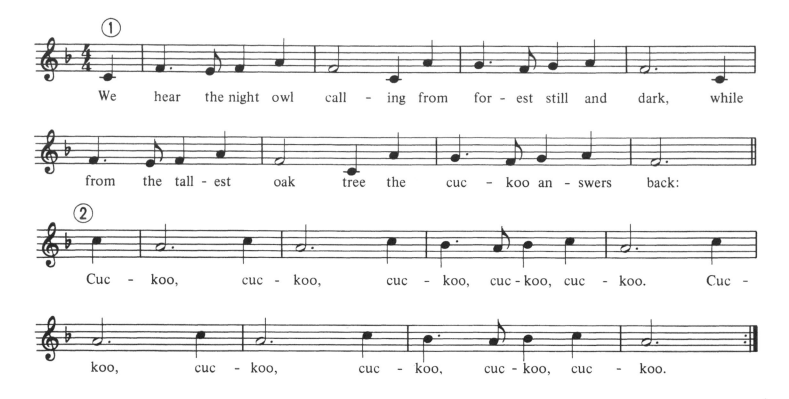

① We hear the night owl call - ing from for - est still and dark, while

from the tall - est oak tree the cuc - koo an - swers back:

② Cuc - koo, cuc - koo, cuc - koo, cuc - koo, cuc - koo. Cuc -

koo, cuc - koo, cuc - koo, cuc - koo, cuc - koo.

Echo Sweet

Warble for us, ech-o sweet, ech-o sweet, Soft-ly now our songs repeat.

Gen - tle ech - o, wake from sleep, Gen - tle ech - o, clear and deep!

Fruitful Fields Are Waving

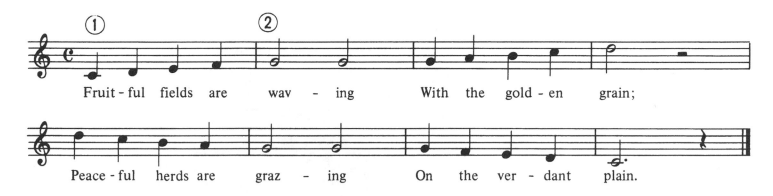

Fruit - ful fields are wav - ing With the gold - en grain;

Peace - ful herds are graz - ing On the ver - dant plain.

Good-Bye

Now we say fare - well, Our pleas - ant work is done; Good-

bye then, good - bye then, all, Un - til to - mor - row's sun.

Here, Where Rippling Waters

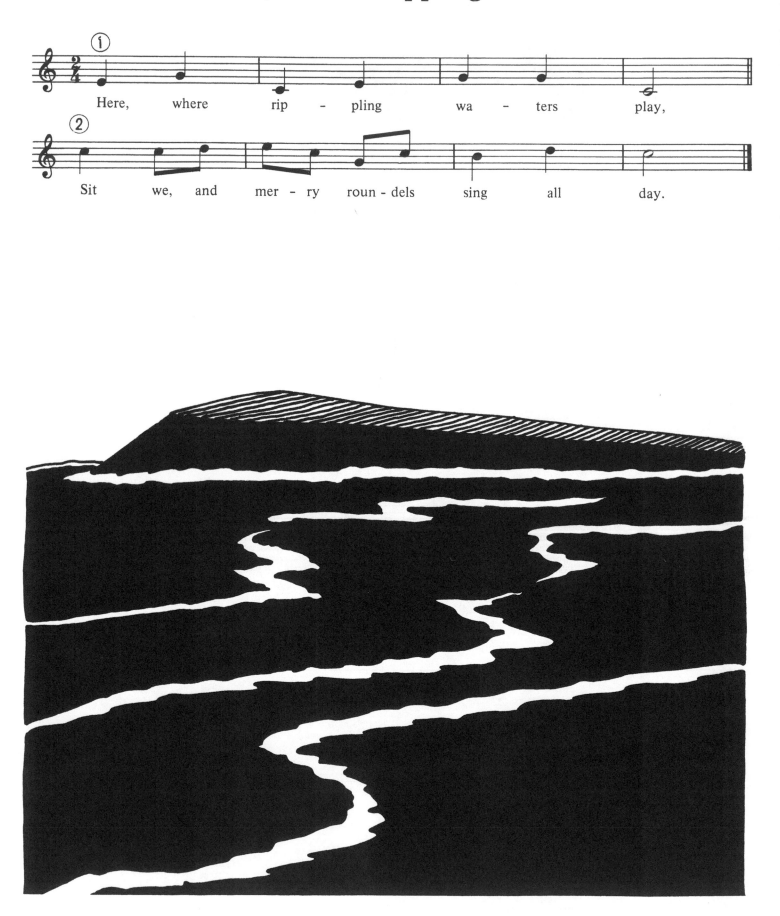

Here, where rip - pling wa - ters play,

Sit we, and mer - ry roun - dels sing all day.

Oh, Give Thanks

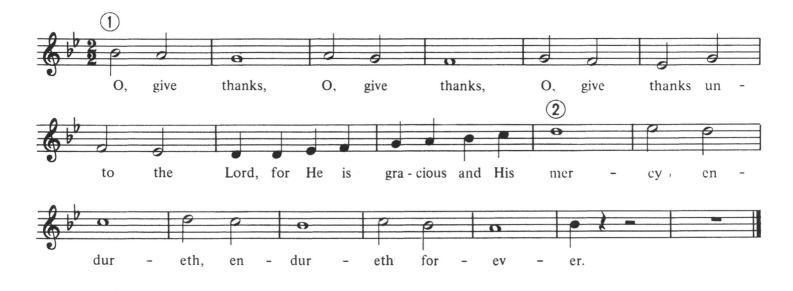

O, give thanks, O, give thanks, O, give thanks un -
to the Lord, for He is gra - cious and His mer - cy en -
dur - eth, en - dur - eth for - ev - er.

Onward, Upward

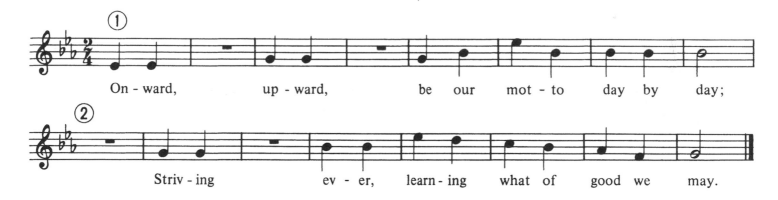

On - ward, up - ward, be our mot - to day by day;

Striv - ing ev - er, learn - ing what of good we may.

Over The Mountain

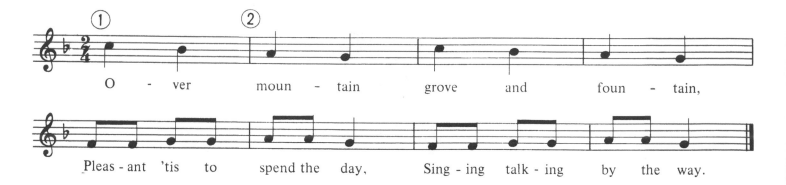

O - ver moun - tain grove and foun - tain,

Pleas - ant 'tis to spend the day, Sing - ing talk - ing by the way.

Past Ten O'Clock

Past ten o' - clock, Fair is the night;

Past ten o' - clock, stars shin - ing bright.

Wake Up! Wake Up!

① Wake___ up! Wake___ up! Proud chan - ti - cleer cries.

② In gold - en glo - ry see the sun rise.

Water Falling

① Wa - ter fall - ing day by___ day wears the

② hard - est rock a - way, Wears the hard - est rock a - way.

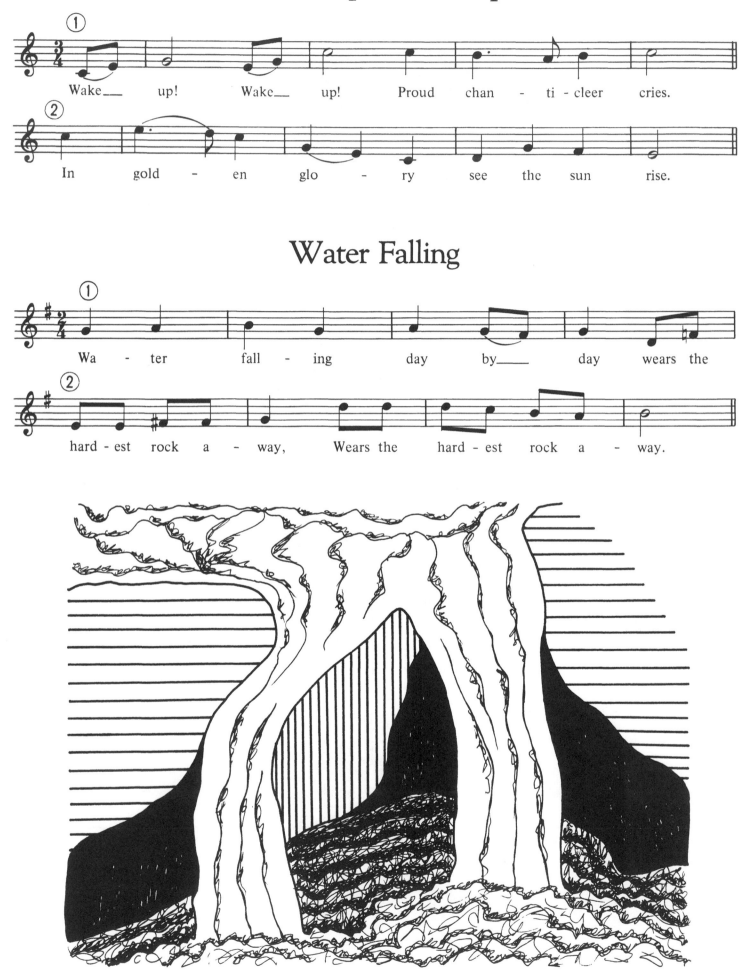

Whether You Whisper Low

Wheth-er you whis-per low, Or wheth-er you loud-ly call, Dis-
tinct-ly, dis-tinct-ly speak, Or do not speak at all.

THREE PART ROUNDS

All In A Fairy Ring

All in a fair-y ring,

Lo! wee folk dance and sing,

Each dew-y May morn-ing.

All Work And No Play

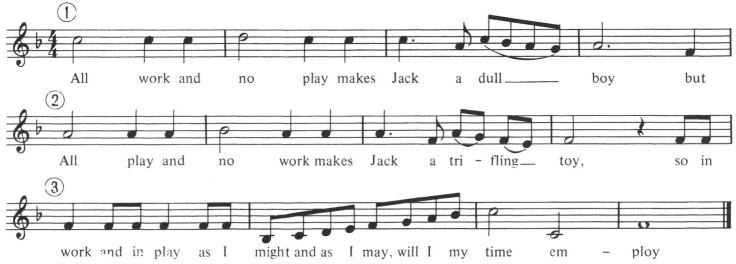

All work and no play makes Jack a dull_____ boy but

All play and no work makes Jack a tri-fling_____ toy, so in

work and in play as I might and as I may, will I my time em - ploy

At Summer Morn

At sum - mer morn the mer - ry lark her - alds in the day. At
e - ven -tide sad Phil-o - mel breathes her plain - tive lay,
War - bling sweet - ly all her grief a - way.

Beauty's But An Idle Boast

Beaut - y's but an i - dle boast;
Yours to - day; to - mor - row lost,
Yours to - day, to - mor - row lost.

The Bell Doth Toll

The bell doth toll, its ech - oes roll, I know the sound full well;
I love its ring-ing, for it calls to sing-ing with its bim, bim, bim, bom, bell.
Bom, Bom, Bom; bim, bome, bell.

Birds Are Singing

A Boat, A Boat!

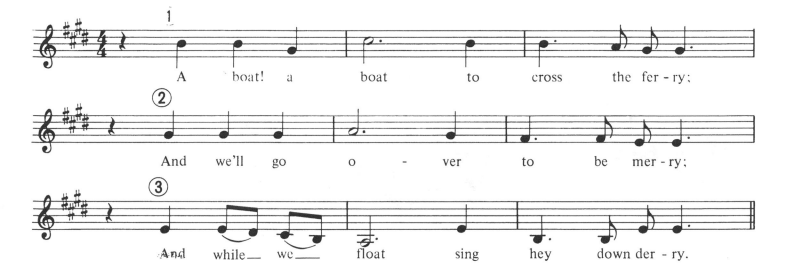

A boat! a boat to cross the fer-ry;

And we'll go o - ver to be mer-ry;

And while we float sing hey down der-ry.

BOW WOW WOW

Bow Wow Wow

My lit - tle dog can no - thing say but bow wow,

wow wow wow, Wow wow wow, what - ev - er he knows

where'- ere he goes, Bow wow wow, wow wow wow.

Bring In The Tea Tray

Bring the tea tray, bring the tea tray, with the milk and the sug-ar and bring in the bread and the but-ter, see that the wa-ter is boil — — ing.

Buy My Dainty Fine Beans

Buy my dain-ty fine beans, buy my beans. Buy my dain-ty fine beans, buy my beans. Crab, crab, buy my crab. Crab, crab, buy my crab. Hot, hot, hot mut-ton pies. Hot, hot mut-ton pies.

Call John

① Call John, the Boat - man Call him a - gain for

loud roars the temp - est and fast falls the rain.

② John is a - sleep, He sleeps ve - ry sound, His

oars___ are at rest, and his boat is a - ground; Loud___

③ ___ roars the ri - ver so rap - id and deep, but the

hard - er you call John, the sound - er he will sleep.

Christmas Is Coming

① Christ - mas is com - ing! The goose is get - ting fat;

② Please to put a pen - ny in the old man's___ hat,

③ Please to put a pen - ny in the old man's hat.

Come Away

Come a - way, Come a - way This is a ve - ry fine

sum - mer's day Come a - way, Come a - way.

Come, Count The Time For Me

Come, count the time for me,_____ come, now, be - gin,

And you shall quick-ly see_____ that thus good time we run;

Now, one, two, three, four, one, two, three, four, one, two, three, four one, two, three.

· ONE · TWO · THREE ·

Come Follow

① Come fol - low fol - low fol - low fol - low, fol - low fol - low me

② With - er shall I fol - low, fol - low, fol - low With - er shall I fol - low, fol - low thee?

③ To the green-wood, to the green - wood, to the green - wood, green - wood tree.

Come And Sing A Merry Song

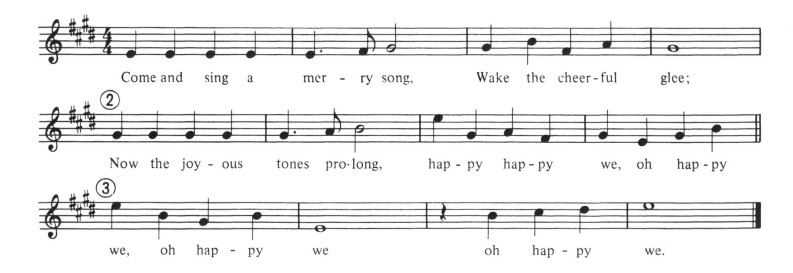

Come and sing a mer - ry song, Wake the cheer - ful glee;

② Now the joy - ous tones pro-long, hap - py hap - py we, oh hap - py

③ we, oh hap - py we oh hap - py we.

Dona Nobis Pacem

Do - na no - bis pa - cem, pa - cem,
Do - na___ no - bis pa - cem. Do -
na no - bis pa - cem, Do - na no - bis
pa - cem. Do - na no - bis___
pa - cem, Do - na no - bis pa - cem.

Glide Along

Glide___ a - long our bon - ny boat, and while with the
tide we gent - ly do float we'll chant to the deep sea's
mel - low - est note, so glide___ a - long our bon - ny boat.___

Grasshoppers Three

① Grass-hop-pers three a – fid-dl-ing went, Hey, ho, ne-ver be still! They

② paid no mo-ney to-ward their rent, but all day long with el – bow bent They

③ fid-dled a tune called Ril-la-by-ril-la-by, Fid-dled a tune called Ril-la-by-rill.

Great Tom Is Cast

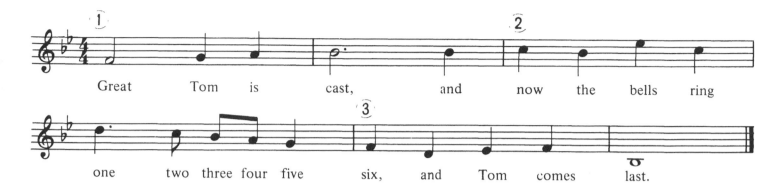

Great Tom is cast, and now the bells ring
one two three four five six, and Tom comes last.

Happy To Meet

Hap - py to meet and sor - ry to part,
Hap - py to meet,___ and sor - ry to part, and hap - py,
hap - py, hap - py hap - py to meet a - gain.

Here I Go

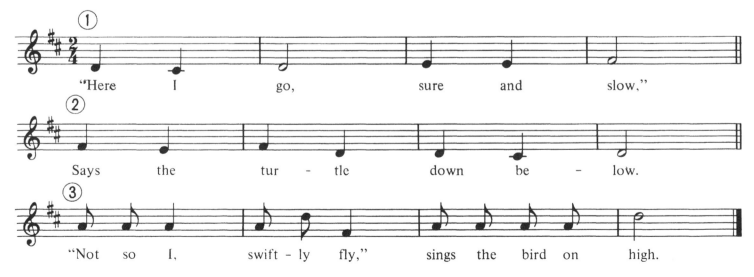

"Here I go, sure and slow,"
Says the tur - tle down be - low.
"Not so I, swift - ly fly," sings the bird on high.

Hey Ho, Nobody's Home

① Hey ho, no - bod - y's home, No meat, nor drink, nor mon-ey have I none,

③ Still I will be mer - ry, ___ Hey ho, no - bod-y's home, No

meat, nor drink, nor mon-ey have I none, Still I will be mer - ry___

Hey ho, no - bod-y's home. ___

Hi! Cheerily Ho

① Hi! Cheer - i - ly, ho, mer - ri - ly, ho,

② Sail - ors are we, sons of the sea, sing - ing with

③ glee. Hi, ho, hi, ho!

Horse To Trot

Horse to trot to trot,___ I say am - ble, and am - ble, and make no stay, Gal - lop, and gal - lop, and gal - lop a - way.

Humpty Dumpty

Hump - ty Dump - ty sat,_____ Hump - ty Dump - ty sat,_____

Hump - ty Dump - ty sat_____ on a wall,

Hump - ty Dump - ty had,_____ Hump - ty Dump - ty had,_____ Hump - ty Dump - ty had_____ a great fall;

All_____ the king's hor - ses, and all_____ the king's men,_____

Could - n't put Hump - ty Dump - ty to - geth - er a - gain.

27

I Am Athirst

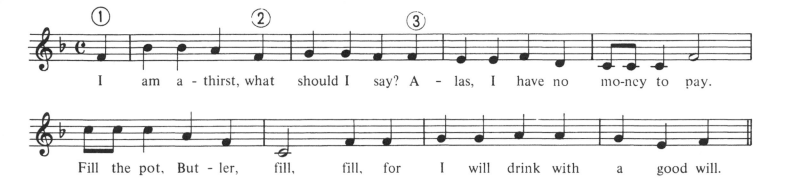

I am a-thirst, what should I say? A-las, I have no mo-ney to pay.

Fill the pot, But-ler, fill, fill, for I will drink with a good will.

If I Know What You Know

If I know what you know and you know what I know, then

I know what you know and you know what I know.

Then I know what you know, then I know what

you know and you know, and you know what I know.

Then I know what you know, and you know what I know,

then I know what you know and you know what I know!

If Thou Tell

If thou_ tell with whom_ thou_ go - est then I'll_ tell thee what_ thou_ do - est for

birds_ of a feath-er ev - er flock to-geth-er, for birds_ of a feath-er ev - er flock to-geth-er.

Joy And Temperance

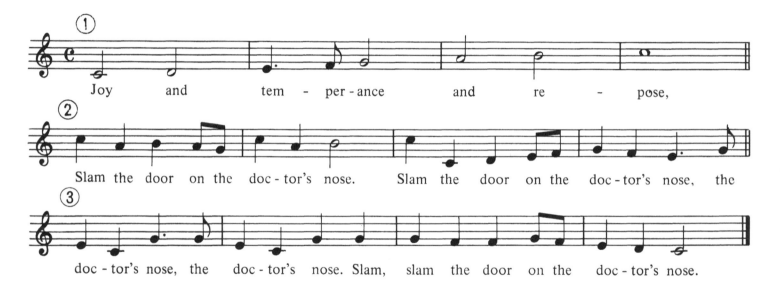

Joy and tem - per - ance and re - pose,

Slam the door on the doc - tor's nose. Slam the door on the doc - tor's nose, the

doc - tor's nose, the doc - tor's nose. Slam, slam the door on the doc - tor's nose.

Laughter Makes The World Go Round

Laugh - ter makes the world_ go _ round,_ so the wise men say.

Laugh - ter is the re - ci - pe to make us all feel gay:

Ha, ha, ha, ha, ha, ha, ha, ha, ho, ho, ho, ho, ho, ho, ho.

Little Miss Muffet

Lit-tle Miss Muf-fet sat on a tuf-fet, Eat-ing her curds and whey; There came a great spi-der, And sat down be-side her, And fright-end Miss Muf-fet a - way. How hor-rid of the spi-der, That ver - y nas-ty spi - der, To fright-en Miss Muf-fet a - way! Oh!

Man's Life

Man's life's a va - pour, full of woes. He cuts a ca - per - down he goes. Down he, down he, down he, down he, down he goes!

The Merry Bells of Hamburg Town

The mer - ry bells of Ham - burg town, To old and young a - like have rung, A din-gle, din-gle, din-gle, din-gle, ding, dang, dong.

The Millwheel

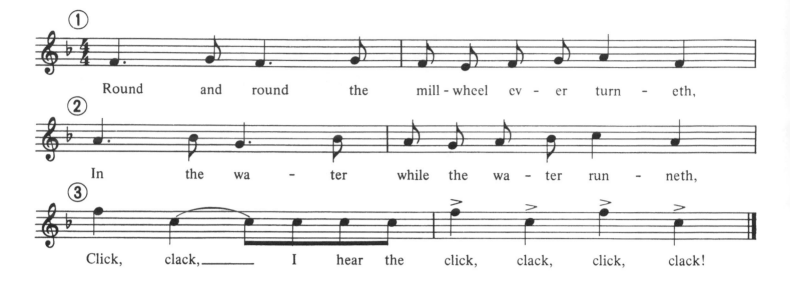

① Round and round the mill-wheel ev - er turn - eth,

② In the wa - ter while the wa - ter run - neth,

③ Click, clack,_____ I hear the click, clack, click, clack!

Morning Papers

① Morn - ing pa - pers, morn - ing pa - pers, ② All the ri - ots,

rows, and ca - pers; ③ "Times," "Dai - ly News."

Not Too Great

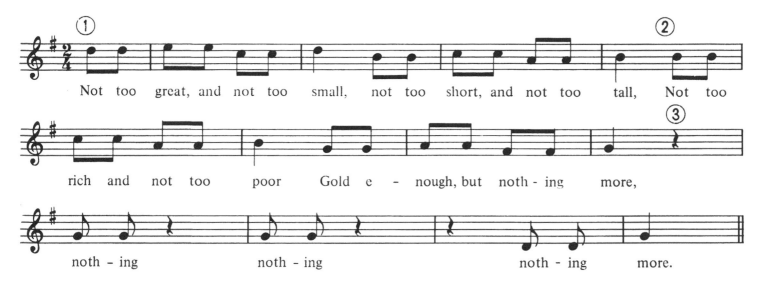

Not too great, and not too small, not too short, and not too tall, Not too
rich and not too poor Gold e - nough, but noth - ing more,
noth - ing noth - ing noth - ing more.

Now The Sun Sinks

Now the sun sinks in_____ the west, aft - er la - bor
com - eth_ rest; Now the sun sinks in_____ the west,
Aft - er la - bor com - eth_ rest; now the sun sinks_____
_____ in the west,_____ Aft - er la - bor com - eth rest.

O How Lovely Is The Evening

O how love - ly is the e - ve - ning, is the eve - ning, When to rest the birds are steal - ing, bells are peal - ing, Ding dong, Ding dong, Ding dong.

Packing Up

Pack - ing up, go - ing a - way O come a - gain___ an - oth - er day O come a - gain___ an - oth - er day, Come a - gain, Come a - gain.

Sandy McNab

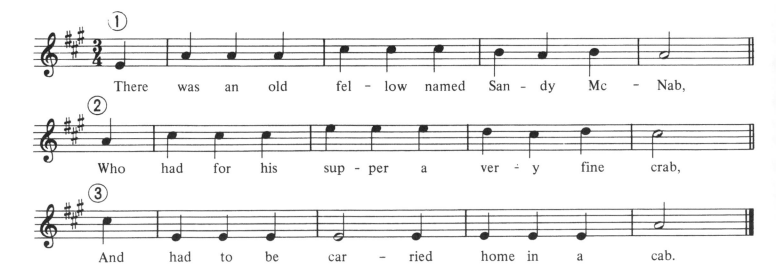

There was an old fel - low named San - dy Mc - Nab,

Who had for his sup - per a ver - y fine crab,

And had to be car - ried home in a cab.

Shut The Door

① Shut the door, if you please Shut the door, Shut the door

② Shut the door, if you please, Shut the door, Shut the door;

③ For the air is grow-ing cold-er I feel it on my shoul-der.

Sing We Now Our Morning Song

① Day is break-ing o'er the hills, Dawn-ing on the lit-tle rills;

② Rouse ye, broth-ers, sis-ters all,___ Cheer-i-ly to each oth-er call, Good

③ morn-ing! Good morn-ing! Good morn-ing! Good morn-ing! Good morn-ing!

Spring Is Coming

① Spring is com-ing quick-ly com-ing haste we now a-way,

② Spring is com-ing, quick-ly com-ing haste we now a-way,

③ O do not stay, nor long de-lay.

Sweetly Sings The Donkey

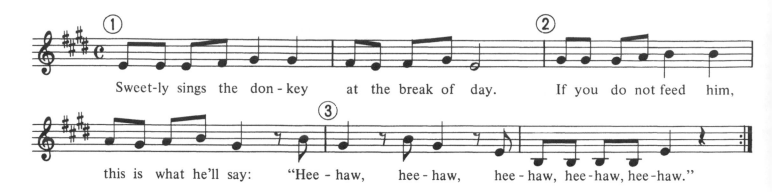

Sweet-ly sings the don-key at the break of day. If you do not feed him,

this is what he'll say: "Hee - haw, hee - haw, hee - haw, hee -haw, hee -haw."

They March, They March

They march, they march to the roll - ing drum; The

sol - diers bold, see! They come, they come to the r - r - roll - ing drum!

Three Bulls And A Bear

Three bulls and a bear, a cob - bler and a tin - ker,

cob - tin - a cob - bler and a tin - ker

- ler, - ker, a cob - bler and a tin - ker.

We Waited For An Omnibus

① We wait – ed for an om – ni – bus, In which there was no

room for us, No room _____ for us.

② So on we went right well con -tent on foot to go our

work _____ to do, our _____ work _____ to do.

③ And that's the ___ way to ___ save the pay, and do ___ with - out an ___

om – ni - bus, in which_ there_ is no room for us.

When A Weary Task

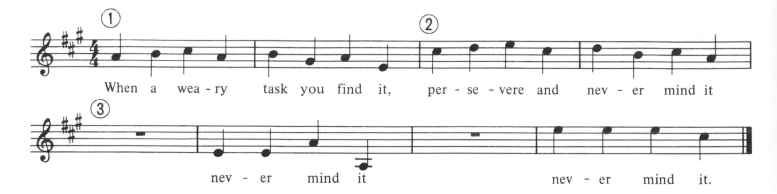

When a wea-ry task you find it, per-se-vere and nev-er mind it

nev-er mind it   nev-er mind it.

When Spring Returns Again

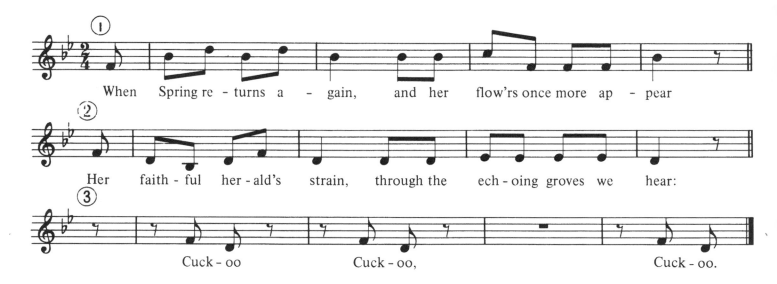

When Spring re-turns a - gain, and her flow'rs once more ap - pear

Her faith-ful her-ald's strain, through the ech-oing groves we hear:

Cuck-oo   Cuck-oo,   Cuck-oo.

Where Is John

Where is John? The old red hen has left her pen.

Where is John? The cows are in the corn a-gain. Oh,

John!_____

White Sand and Grey Sand

White sand and grey sand, Who'll buy my white sand? Who'll buy my grey sand?

Who Comes Laughing?

Who comes laugh-ing, laugh-ing, laugh-ing, who comes laugh-ing here a - gain?

We come laugh-ing, Ha ha ha ha ha ha ha ha, we come laugh-ing here a - gain.

Ha ha ha ha ha ha ha ha, ha ha ha ha ha ha ha ha, ha ha ha ha ha ha ha ha, ha ha ha ha ha!

Ye Sportive Birds

Ye sport - ive birds, in cir - cles high, Your____

fight for - ev - er wing - ing.

And____ ye who____ make the woods more high, All____

vo - cal____ with____ your____ sing - ing.

May joy____ be yours, in____ flight and

song, To - day, and____ long.

FOUR PART ROUNDS

Yes! 'Tis Raining

Yes! 'Tis rain - ing ev - 'ry oth - er morn - ing, Ev' - ry day and ev - 'ry oth - er eve - ning. Rain, rain, go to Spain; Rain, go to Spain!

The Blacksmith

Now the black - smith's arm is swing - ing, And his cheer - ful song he's sing - ing; Kling! Kling! Klang! Klang!

Come, Let's Sing A Merry Round

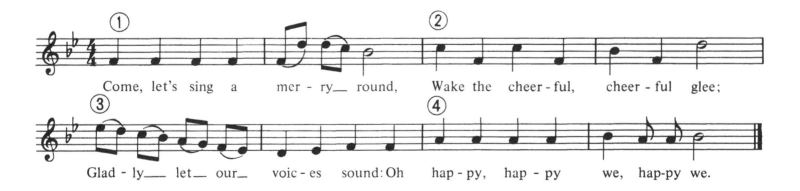

Come, let's sing a mer - ry round, Wake the cheer - ful, cheer - ful glee; Glad - ly let our voic - es sound: Oh hap - py, hap - py we, hap-py we.

Cat In The Plumtree

La - dy, come down and see, the cat sits in the plum tree!

A Cuckoo Catch

The cheer-ful day is dawn - ing, I hear the cuck - oo sing.

To ush - er in the morn - ing, And wel - come gen - tle Spring.

Cuck - oo! cuck - oo! cuck - oo!

I hear the cuck - oo, And wel - come in the___ Spring.

Do, Re, Mi, Fa

Do Re Mi Fa I am tir'd of this sol - fa - ing

I know not what you've been say - ing.

Donkeys Love Carrots

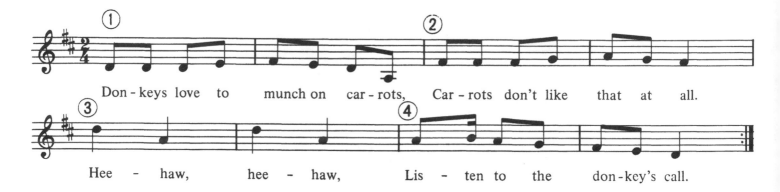

① Don - keys love to munch on car - rots, ② Car - rots don't like that at all.

③ Hee - haw, hee - haw, ④ Lis - ten to the don - key's call.

Frere Jacques

Are you sleep-ing, are you sleep-ing, Bro-ther John, Bro-ther John?

Morn-ing bells are ring-ing, morn-ing bells are ring-ing, Ding ding dong! Ding ding dong!

Frère Jacques, Frère Jacques,
Dormez-vous, dormez-vous?
Sonnez les matines, sonnez les matines,
Ding din don! Ding din don!

The Ghost Of John

Have you seen the ghost of John? Long white bones with the rest all gone,____

Oooh____ Oooh_____ Would-n't it be chil-ly with no skin on?

Good-Morning

Sing we now our morn-ing song, We have sung it

oft and long, Ev-'ry morn 'tis fresh and new As the

pear-ly drops of dew; Good morn-ing! Good morn-ing! Good morn-ing!

Good Night, Good Night

① Good night! Good night! Good night!

② Time sends a warn-ing call, sweet — rest de-scend on all,

③ Time sends its warn-ing call, sweet — rest de-scend on all,

④ Good night, good night!

Haste Makes Waste

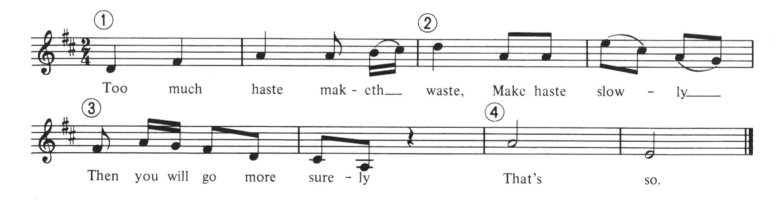

① Too much haste mak-eth — waste, ② Make haste slow – ly —

③ Then you will go more sure – ly ④ That's so.

I'll Begin

① I'll be-gin and you may fol-low now, ② And then may join an-oth-er now,

③ So we'll sing a round to-geth-er keep-ing time and ④ tune both now and ev – er.

Hear The Lively Songs Of The Frogs

Hear the live - ly song of the frogs in yon - der pond:

Krik, krik, krik, krik, krik, krik, Brrrrrr - um!

Jack, Boy, Ho, Boy

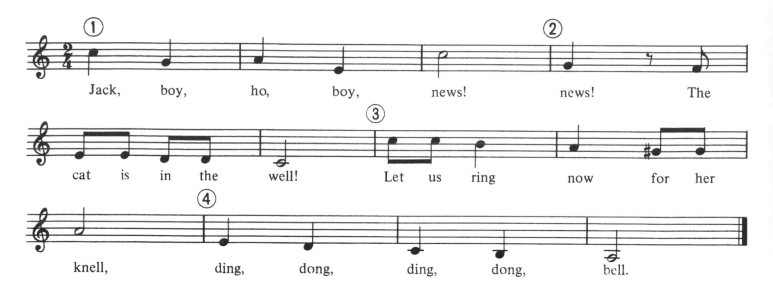

Jack, boy, ho, boy, news! news! The
cat is in the well! Let us ring now for her
knell, ding, dong, ding, dong, bell.

Jane Glover

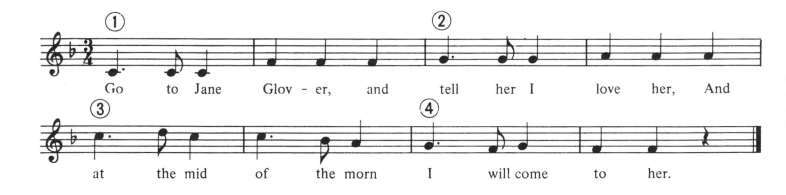

Go to Jane Glov - er, and tell her I love her, And
at the mid of the morn I will come to her.

Jolly Round

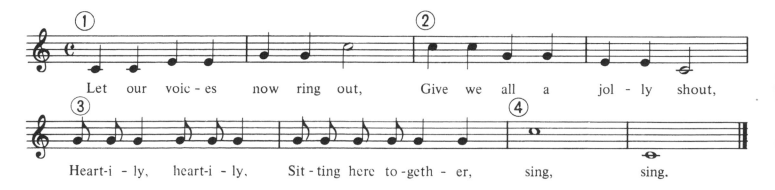

Let our voic - es now ring out, Give we all a jol - ly shout,
Heart-i - ly, heart-i - ly, Sit - ting here to-geth - er, sing, sing.

A Lame, Tame Crane

My dame hath a lame, tame crane, My dame hath a crane that is lame.

Pray gen-tle Jane, let my dame's lame, tame crane feed and come home a - gain.

The Lark, Linnet, And Nightingale

The lark, lin-net and night-in-gale. To sing some say____ are best, Yet

mer - ri - ly sings ____ lit-tle ro-bin, Pret-ty rob-in with the red breast.

Laughing May Is Here

Laugh-ing__ May is here, Blith-est__ of the year;

Hark! Hear the blue-bird_ say: Mer-ry, mer-ry, mer-ry, mer-ry May.

Let The Wind Blow

① Let the wind ② blow, High or low,

③ Still jol-ly tars are we, on ___ the ___ ④ O - cean so free.

May-Day

① 'Tis blithe May - day, ② Come haste a - way! ③ Gay flags are streaming

④ On the vil-lage green, Bright fac-es beam - ing All a-round are seen.

Love Your Neighbor

① Love your neigh - bor ② live by la - bor ③ would you pros - per ④ that's the way.

Merrily, Merrily

Mer-ri-ly, mer-ri-ly   greet the morn,   Chee-ri - ly, cheeri - ly   sound the horn,

Hark! to the ech-oes!   Hear them play O'er hill and dale and   far   a - way.

Merrily, Merrily Greet The Morn

Mer-ri - ly, mer-ri - ly   greet the morn,   Chee-ri - ly, chee-ri - ly   Sound the horn.

Hark to the e - choes, hear them play   O - ver the hills   and far a - way.

Morning Is Come

Morn - ing is   come,   Night is a - way,

Rise with the sun____ And____ wel - come the   day.

My Goose And Thy Goose

Why does-n't my goose sing as well as your goose

when I paid for my goose twice as much as you?

My Paddle's Keen And Bright

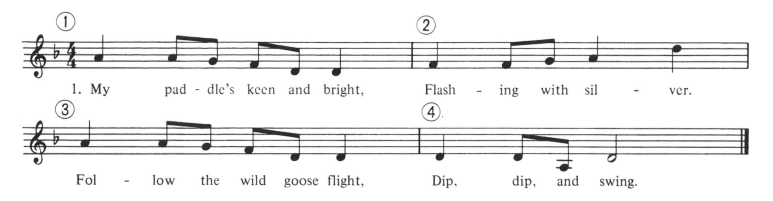

1. My pad - dle's keen and bright, Flash - ing with sil - ver. Fol - low the wild goose flight, Dip, dip, and swing.

2. Dip, dip, and swing her back,
   Flashing with silver.
   Swift as the wild goose flies,
   Dip, dip, and swing.

Now The Day Is Nearly Done

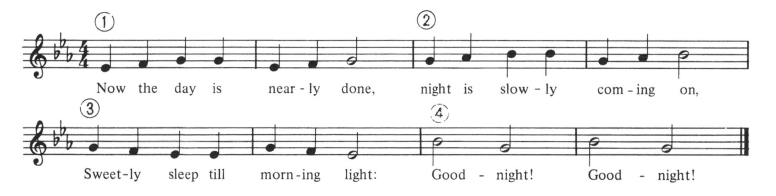

Now the day is near - ly done, night is slow - ly com - ing on, Sweet - ly sleep till morn - ing light: Good - night! Good - night!

Now We'll Make The Rafters Ring

Now we'll make the raft - ers ring, while we all this round will sing.

On Mules We Find

① On mules we find two legs be-hind, and two we find be - fore.

② We stand be - hind be fore we find what the two be - hind be - for.

③ When we're be - hind the two be - hind, we find what these be - for.

④ So stand be - fore the two be - hind, and be - hind the two be - fore.

Row, Row, Row Your Boat

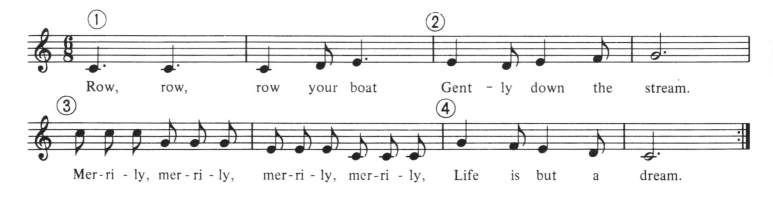

① Row, row, row your boat ② Gent - ly down the stream.

③ Mer-ri - ly, mer - ri - ly, mer-ri - ly, mer-ri - ly, ④ Life is but a dream.

Sing It Over

① Sing it o - ver ② With your might;

③ Ne - ver leave it, ne - ver leave it ④ Till 'tis right.

Scotland's Burning

① ②
Scot - land's burn - ing, Scot - land's burn - ing! Look out! look out!

③ ④
Fire! fire! fire! fire! Pour on wa - ter, pour on wa - ter!

Those Evening Bells

① Those even-ing bells, those even-ing bells, How man-y tales their mu-sic tells.

② Of youth and home and that sweet time When first we heard their sooth-ing chime.

③ Those ring-ing, jing ling even-ing bells, How man-y tales their mu-sic tells.

④ Those even-ing bells, those evening bells, How man-y tales their mu-sic tells.

Thou Poor Bird

① Thou poor bird, Take thy flight, Where
Thou poor bird, mourn'st thy the tree, Where

③ far a - bove the sor - rows of this sad night.
sweet - ly thou - didst war - ble in thy wand'r - ings free.

Sing One, Two, Three

Sing one, two, three, Come fol - low me, And so shall we Good fel - lows _ be.

Sweet Is The Hour

Sweet is the hour of twi - light grey, When eve - ning veils the face of day; When shades __ of night be - gin to fall, The dark - ness soon will cov - er all.

Thirty Days Hath September

Thir - ty days hath Sep - tem - ber, A - pril, June, and No - vem - ber, All the rest have thir - ty - one, Sa - ving Feb - ru - a - ry, a - lone, Which has twen - ty - eight, rain or shine, And on leap year twen - ty - nine.

Three Blind Mice

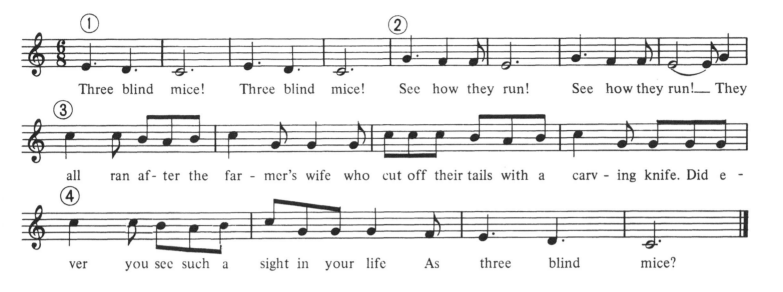

Three blind mice! Three blind mice! See how they run! See how they run!__ They all ran af-ter the far - mer's wife who cut off their tails with a carv - ing knife. Did e - ver you see such a sight in your life As three blind mice?

Wake And Sing

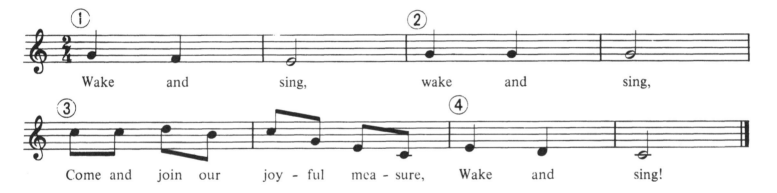

Wake and sing, wake and sing, Come and join our joy - ful mea - sure, Wake and sing!

Well Rung, Tom

Well rung, Tom, boy, well rung, Tom, Ding-dong, cuck-oo, well rung, Tom. The owl and the cuck-oo, the fool and the song, Well sung, cuck - oo, well rung, Tom.

Where Are You Going, My Pretty Maid

White Coral Bells

The White Hen

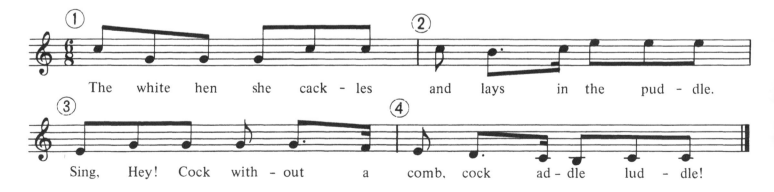

Who'll Buy My Posies

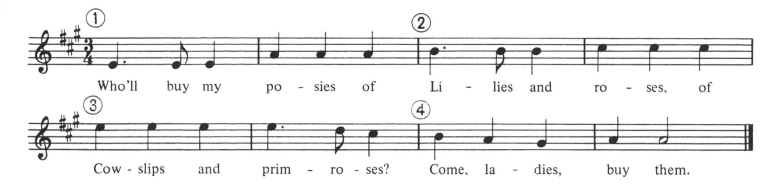

Who'll buy my po - sies of Li - lies and ro - ses, of
Cow - slips and prim - ro - ses? Come, la - dies, buy them.

FIVE PART ROUNDS

Jinkin The Jester

Jin - kin the jest - er was wont to make glee with
Jar - vis the jug - gler till an - gry was he. Then
Wil - kin the wise man did wise - ly fore - see that
jug - gler and jest - er should gent - ly a - gree.
Hey down, down, down, down, der - ry - down, down, der - ry - down, down.

Sing Together Merrily

Sing to - geth - er mer - ri - ly, mer - ri - ly sing, mer - ri - ly, mer - ri - ly sing,

Mer - ri - ly, mer - ri - ly, mer - ri - ly, mer - ri - ly sing!

SIX PART ROUNDS

Thirty Days Hath September

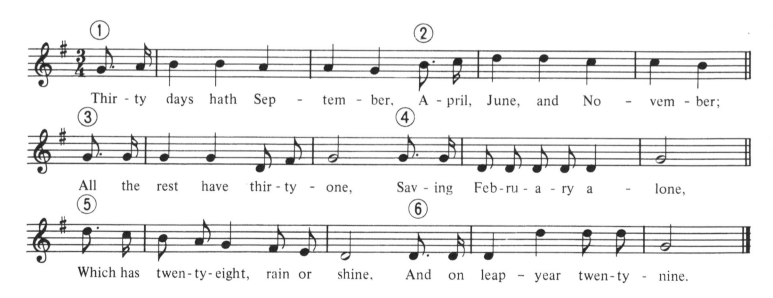

Thir - ty days hath Sep - tem - ber, A - pril, June, and No - vem - ber;

All the rest have thir - ty - one, Sav - ing Feb - ru - a - ry a - lone,

Which has twen - ty - eight, rain or shine, And on leap - year twen - ty - nine.

EIGHT PART ROUNDS

Laughing May Is Here

Laugh-ing May is here, Blith-est of the year; Hark! hear the blue-bird say: Mer-ry, mer-ry, mer-ry, mer-ry May.

Little Bo-Peep

Lit-tle Bo-Peep has lost her sheep, and can-not tell where to find them, Leave them a-lone and they'll come home, and bring their tails be-hind them.